U.S. FISH AND WILDLIFE SERVICE
TAKE PRIDE IN CHESAPEAKE BAY

The Chesapeake Bay is the largest estuary in North America. Its waters provide food and habitat for an abundance of fish and wildlife. It serves as a highway for commerce, a playground for the public, a storehouse of food, and a home for over 13 million people who live in its vast watershed. But in recent years the Chesapeake has become less able to support the fish and wildlife it once did. Increasing amounts of nutrients, sediments, and toxic substances are causing serious ecological problems in the Bay. Studies show alarming declines in populations of fish and wildlife and in the habitat available to them.

The U.S. Fish and Wildlife Service is one of many Federal, State, and local agencies and private organizations engaged in the Chesapeake Bay restoration program. Together they are working to reverse the damage already done, to arrest further degradation and to restore the Bay to its former productivity as nearly as time, technology and resources allow.

Art by David Folker
Verse by Jamie Harms

Reprint 1993

 Recycled paper

Chessie

A CHESAPEAKE BAY STORY

CHESSIE

For at least half a century people have reported seeing a "sea monster" in the Chesapeake Bay. Affectionately known as "Chessie," popularized cousin of Nessie (Scotland's Loch Ness monster), the creature is reported to be gentle and good natured.

What Chessie really is and whether this Chesapeake phenomenon actually exists is a matter of speculation—but Chessie does exist in the following pages with an important message for everyone who values the natural heritage of the Chesapeake Bay. Our fictional character Chessie represents all those creatures that depend on the Bay for food and habitat.

I'm Chessie, the monster of
Chesapeake Bay.
I'm not very scary—
I stay out of the way,
And some people don't believe
I'm even there.
But I am—as you see—
with a story to share.

I swim in the Bay,
from the north to the south,
From its freshwater streams
to its saltwater mouth;
For *two hundred miles*
between its two ends,
The Bay is my home
and the home of my friends.

We all live together
in Chesapeake waters:
The catfish and rockfish,
the muskrats and otters,
The oysters and crabs,
the minnows and eels,
With our neighbors—
bald eagles, black ducks,
wigeons, and teals.

And plenty of people—
by the *millions*—come in
To fish or catch oysters,
to sail or to swim.
They bring in their freighters
and build on the shore.
Each year there seem to be
more, **more, more, more** . . .

People! I love them,
but oh, what a mess
They can make with their projects.
Sometimes, I confess,
My patience gets thin.
They don't think for a minute
how the Bay will survive
when they dump so much in it.

So the Bay's become dirty.
It's mucky and brown
From the poisons that come
from each factory and town.
The oil, soil, and trash
that pour in it each day
May force us to leave,
BUT we'd much rather stay!

So we've got to clean up
if we want to be sure
To have seafood to eat
from water that's pure.
And we've got to start NOW—
there's no time to wait.
Things will only get worse,
until it's *too late!*

Who's going to clean up?
Well, it has to be *you*,
And your parents and friends
and your neighbors. *Me*, too!
Whoever likes having the Bay here—
that's who.
We *all* have to help.
Here's some things *you* can do.

Obey fishing laws.
Take what you need and no more.
Pick up the litter
and trash on the shore.
And *never* put anything
into the Bay
That might hurt me
or my friends in some way.

That's all of my story.
Now I've got to hurry
And tell all my animal
friends not to worry.
We'll get the job done,
day by day, week by week,
And together we'll bring back
the rich Chesapeake.

Related publications available through the Chesapeake Bay Field Office

Chessie Returns:
A sequel coloring book/story about Chessie, the friendly Bay Monster, which highlights human development as a problem for the Bay and provides a conservation message. Pub. by USFWS.

Bay BC's:
A multi-disciplinary approach to teaching about the Chesapeake Bay. Bay BC'S includes background material and lesson plans for teachers of grades K-3, with songs, games and stories for students. Pub. By USFWS, & Dept. of Education and Interpretation, National Aquarium in Baltimore.

Changing Chesapeake:
A multi-disciplinary approach to teaching about the Chesapeake Bay. Changing Chesapeake includes background material and lesson plans for teachers of grades K-3, with songs, games, and stories for students. Pub. by USFWS, and Dept. of Education and Interpretation, National Aquarium in Baltimore.

Watershed Activity Kit:
A three part kit: A non- technical Bay watershed map emphasizing the immense network of rivers and streams that make up the Chesapeake drainage system, student work maps, and a teacher guide.

U.S. Fish and Wildlife Service
Chesapeake Bay Field Office
177 Admiral Cochrane Drive
Annapolis, MD 21401
410-573-4593
410-573-4500

As one of the primary Federal stewards of the nation's living resources, the U.S. Fish and Wildlife Service provides leadership in habitat and wetlands protection, fish and wildlife research, technical assistance, and in the conservation and protection of migratory birds, anadromous fishes, certain marine mammals, and endangered species. The Service manages 492 National Wildlife Refuges encompassing over 88 million acres and 81 National Fish Hatcheries across the country, including several in the Bay area.